Simple Rough Drafts Workbook

Trackable Progress

K-3 Short Compositions Practice Workbook 2 of 3

SherLynne Beach, SuccessFamilies

Simply Rough Drafts Workbook
Trackable Progress
K-3 Short Compositions Practice Workbook 2 of 3
By SherLynne Beach, SuccessFamilies
Copyright 2015 SherLynne Beach and SuccessFamilies

ISBN-13: 978-1517108366
ISBN-10: 1517108365

Dedication

1

To my children's success, and your children's.

To my mother, dedicated editor, great parent and grandparent, wonderful friend.

To my husband…ibid, forever.

Table of Contents

Date	Title	Page
		11
		15
		19
		23
		27
		31
		35
		39
		43
		47
		51
		55
		59
		63
		67
		71
		75
		79
		83
		87
		91
		95
		99
		103

Introduction

I created the Writing Steps Series Workbooks to assist my children in becoming proficient writers. These workbooks can be used with any writing program, though I made them to use with my children's Institute for Excellence in Writing programs.

There are three books in the series – Outlines, Rough Drafts, and Final Copies Each book has enough room for 60 writing projects, one for each week of the year, plus a few extra. This Rough Draft Workbook even includes expandable word lists to help budding writers choose interesting words.

As the homeschooling mom that I am, I found this system to be quite helpful…something a little more formal to keep writing a special and respected activity…no more lost drafts in odd notebooks scattered around the house or lost time repairing holes of hole-punched writing paper. I can also quickly flip through the books with my children and, together, see the progress made over time.

I hope you find these useful and enjoy them as we do!

Rough Draft Instructions

- **FIRST DRAFT**

    o Using Your Outline only, write the paragraph.

- **REVISE (follow your course instructions)**

    o Add sentences or words to make it more interesting.

    o Remove words or sentences you don't need

    o Move words or sentences if you need to.

    o Substitute – trade words or sentences for new one.

- **EDIT and PROOF READ**

    o Capitalize – First letters of sentences, Proper nouns,

    o Check if nouns and verbs are used properly

    o Check to see that punctuation is used correctly.

    o Spelling – check for homophones – use a dictionary or a thesaurus.

- **Move onto the next book –FINAL COPY.**

Rough Draft

DATE:____

TITLE:____

Write the first draft. Revise. Edit. Proof Read.

Rough Draft

DATE:____

TITLE:____ .

Write the first draft. Revise. Edit. Proof Read.

Rough Draft

DATE:____

TITLE:____

Write the first draft. Revise. Edit. Proof Read.

Rough Draft

DATE:_______________________________________

TITLE:______________________________________

Write the first draft. Revise. Edit. Proof Read.

Rough Draft

DATE:_______________________________________

TITLE:_______________________________________

Write the first draft. Revise. Edit. Proof Read.

Rough Draft

DATE:_______________________________________

TITLE:_______________________________________

Write the first draft. Revise. Edit. Proof Read.

____

____

____

____

____

____

____

____

____

____

Rough Draft

DATE:____

TITLE:____

Write the first draft. Revise. Edit. Proof Read.

Rough Draft

DATE:____

TITLE:____

Write the first draft. Revise. Edit. Proof Read.

Rough Draft

DATE:____

TITLE:____

Write the first draft. Revise. Edit. Proof Read.

____

____

____

____

____

____

____

____

____

Rough Draft

DATE:_______________________________________

TITLE:______________________________________

Write the first draft. Revise. Edit. Proof Read.

Rough Draft

DATE:____

TITLE:____

Write the first draft. Revise. Edit. Proof Read.

Rough Draft

DATE:____

TITLE:____

Write the first draft. Revise. Edit. Proof Read.

Rough Draft

DATE:____

TITLE:____

Write the first draft. Revise. Edit. Proof Read.

Rough Draft

DATE:_______________________________________

TITLE:______________________________________

Write the first draft. Revise. Edit. Proof Read.

Rough Draft

DATE:_______________________________________

TITLE:_______________________________________

Write the first draft. Revise. Edit. Proof Read.

Rough Draft

DATE:____

TITLE:____

Write the first draft. Revise. Edit. Proof Read.

Rough Draft

DATE:_______________________________________

TITLE:_______________________________________

Write the first draft. Revise. Edit. Proof Read.

Rough Draft

DATE:___________________________________

TITLE:__________________________________

Write the first draft. Revise. Edit. Proof Read.

Rough Draft

DATE:___________________________________

TITLE:___________________________________

Write the first draft. Revise. Edit. Proof Read.

Rough Draft

DATE:____

TITLE:______________________________________

Write the first draft. Revise. Edit. Proof Read.

Rough Draft

DATE:____

TITLE:____

Write the first draft. Revise. Edit. Proof Read.

Rough Draft

DATE:____

TITLE:____

Write the first draft. Revise. Edit. Proof Read.

Rough Draft

DATE:_______________________________________

TITLE:______________________________________

Write the first draft. Revise. Edit. Proof Read.

Rough Draft

DATE:____

TITLE:____

Write the first draft. Revise. Edit. Proof Read.

Rough Draft

DATE:____

TITLE:____

Write the first draft. Revise. Edit. Proof Read.

Rough Draft

DATE:____

TITLE:____

Write the first draft. Revise. Edit. Proof Read.

Rough Draft

DATE:____

TITLE:_______________________________________

Write the first draft. Revise. Edit. Proof Read.

Rough Draft

DATE:_______________________________________

TITLE:______________________________________

Write the first draft. Revise. Edit. Proof Read.

Rough Draft

DATE:____

TITLE:____

Write the first draft. Revise. Edit. Proof Read.

Rough Draft

DATE:_______________________________________

TITLE:_______________________________________

Write the first draft. Revise. Edit. Proof Read.

Rough Draft

DATE:____

TITLE:____

Write the first draft. Revise. Edit. Proof Read.

Rough Draft

DATE:____

TITLE:____

Write the first draft. Revise. Edit. Proof Read.

Rough Draft

DATE:_______________________________________

TITLE:______________________________________

Write the first draft. Revise. Edit. Proof Read.

Rough Draft

DATE:______________________________________

TITLE:____________________________________

Write the first draft. Revise. Edit. Proof Read.

Rough Draft

DATE:____

TITLE:____

Write the first draft. Revise. Edit. Proof Read.

Rough Draft

DATE:____

TITLE:____

Write the first draft. Revise. Edit. Proof Read.

Rough Draft

DATE:____

TITLE:____

Write the first draft. Revise. Edit. Proof Read.

Rough Draft

DATE:____

TITLE:____

Write the first draft. Revise. Edit. Proof Read.

Rough Draft

DATE:____

TITLE:____

Write the first draft. Revise. Edit. Proof Read.

Rough Draft

DATE:_______________________________________

TITLE:______________________________________

Write the first draft. Revise. Edit. Proof Read.

Rough Draft

DATE:____

TITLE:____

Write the first draft. Revise. Edit. Proof Read.

____

____

____

____

____

____

____

____

____

Rough Draft

DATE:_______________________________________

TITLE:_______________________________________

Write the first draft. Revise. Edit. Proof Read.

Rough Draft

DATE:______________________________________

TITLE:____________________________________

Write the first draft. Revise. Edit. Proof Read.

Rough Draft

DATE:_______________________________________

TITLE:_______________________________________

Write the first draft. Revise. Edit. Proof Read.

Rough Draft

DATE:____

TITLE:____

Write the first draft. Revise. Edit. Proof Read.

Rough Draft

DATE:____

TITLE:____

Write the first draft. Revise. Edit. Proof Read.

Rough Draft

DATE:_______________________________________

TITLE:_______________________________________

Write the first draft. Revise. Edit. Proof Read.

Rough Draft

DATE:_______________________________________

TITLE:______________________________________

Write the first draft. Revise. Edit. Proof Read.

Rough Draft

DATE:_______________________________________

TITLE:______________________________________

Write the first draft. Revise. Edit. Proof Read.

Rough Draft

DATE:____

TITLE:____

Write the first draft. Revise. Edit. Proof Read.

____

____

____

____

____

____

____

____

____

____

Rough Draft

DATE:____

TITLE:____

Write the first draft. Revise. Edit. Proof Read.

Rough Draft

DATE:____

TITLE:____

Write the first draft. Revise. Edit. Proof Read.

Rough Draft

DATE:____

TITLE:____

Write the first draft. Revise. Edit. Proof Read.

Rough Draft

DATE:_______________________________________

TITLE:______________________________________

Write the first draft. Revise. Edit. Proof Read.

____

____

____

____

____

____

____

____

____

Rough Draft

DATE:____

TITLE:____

Write the first draft. Revise. Edit. Proof Read.

Rough Draft

DATE:_______________________________________

TITLE:_______________________________________

Write the first draft. Revise. Edit. Proof Read.

Rough Draft

DATE:_______________________________________

TITLE:_______________________________________

Write the first draft. Revise. Edit. Proof Read.

Rough Draft

DATE:_____________________________________

TITLE:_____________________________________

Write the first draft. Revise. Edit. Proof Read.

Rough Draft

DATE:____

TITLE:____

Write the first draft. Revise. Edit. Proof Read.

Rough Draft

DATE:_______________________________________

TITLE:_______________________________________

Write the first draft. Revise. Edit. Proof Read.

Rough Draft

DATE:____

TITLE:____

Write the first draft. Revise. Edit. Proof Read.

Rough Draft

DATE:_____________________________________

TITLE:_____________________________________

Write the first draft. Revise. Edit. Proof Read.

Rough Draft

DATE:_______________________________________

TITLE:______________________________________

Write the first draft. Revise. Edit. Proof Read.

Rough Draft

DATE:_______________________________________

TITLE:______________________________________

Write the first draft. Revise. Edit. Proof Read.

____

____

____

____

____

____

____

____

____

____

Rough Draft

DATE:_______________________________________

TITLE:______________________________________

Write the first draft. Revise. Edit. Proof Read.

Amazing Words

Lists of words to enliven your writing!

<u>BANNED WORDS</u>

Avoid using these words.

Try using another that describes what you want to say even better than one of these words.

-Use the lists of ideas (and add to these lists!)

Go	Say	Pretty	big
Went	Said	Bad	
Come	Mean	Ugly	
Came	Nice	Good	

Great Adjectives: GOOD

How many more words can you add?

agreeable	friendly	obliging	suited
apt	generous	pleasant	superior
capable	gracious	proper	wonderful
excellent	kindly	qualified	
fine	marvelous	suitable	

Great Adjectives: PRETTY

How many more words can you come up with?

adorable	captivating	elegant	magnificent
appealing	classy	enchanting	splendid
attractive	dazzling	gorgeous	superb
beautiful	divine	lovely	

Great Adjectives: NICE

How many more words can you come up with?

admirable	courteous	helpful	pleasant
agreeable	decent	kind	polite
appealing	delightful	likeable	right
attractive	effective	lovely	satisfy
charming	flattering		
considerate	friendly		

Great Adjectives: INTERESTING

How many more words can you come up with?

amusing	delightful	enthralling	intriguing
appealing	enchanting	exciting	riveting
attractive	engaging	fascinating	spell binding
captivating	engrossing	gripping	stirring
compelling	entertaining	impressive	

Great Adjectives: BIG

How many more words can you come up with?

ample	great	sizable	titanic
astronomical	huge	spacious	tremendous
broad	large	stout	
expansive	mammoth	substantial	
grand	mountainous	tall	

Great Adjectives: BAD

How many more words can you come up with?

despicable	incorrect	rotten	wretched
disagreeable	lousy	spoiled	wrong
dreadful	mean	terrible	
foul	mean	unruly	
horrible	poor	vile	

Great Adjectives: UGLY

How many more words can you come up with?

appalling	disfigured	hideous	revolting
awful	disgusting	offensive	unattractive
awful	gross	repulsive	unsightly

<u>Great Adjectives: MEAN</u>

How many more words can you come up with?

brutal	heartless	ruthless	violent
cruel	hostile	savage	wicked
evil	merciless	sinister	
ferocious	nasty	vicious	

Great Verbs: GO/WENT/CAME/COME

How many more words can you add?

arrive	escape	leave	travelled
depart	exit	proceed	traversed
depart	fade	ran	visited
disappear	flee	travel	walked

Great Verbs: <u>TELL/SAY/SAID</u>

How many more words can you add?

advise	inform	sigh	swear
announce	mutter	sing	thunder
assure	negate	snarl	voice
content	notify	snort	vow
direct	recount	squawk	whisper
dispute	relate	stammer	yelp
grunt	remark	state	

<u>Favorite Words</u>

How many words can you add?

	282	

283		

For **More & Longer Great Word Lists**

Get the book-

"Useful Word Lists for Young Writers"

By SherLynne Beach

Coming Fall 2019